D1129880

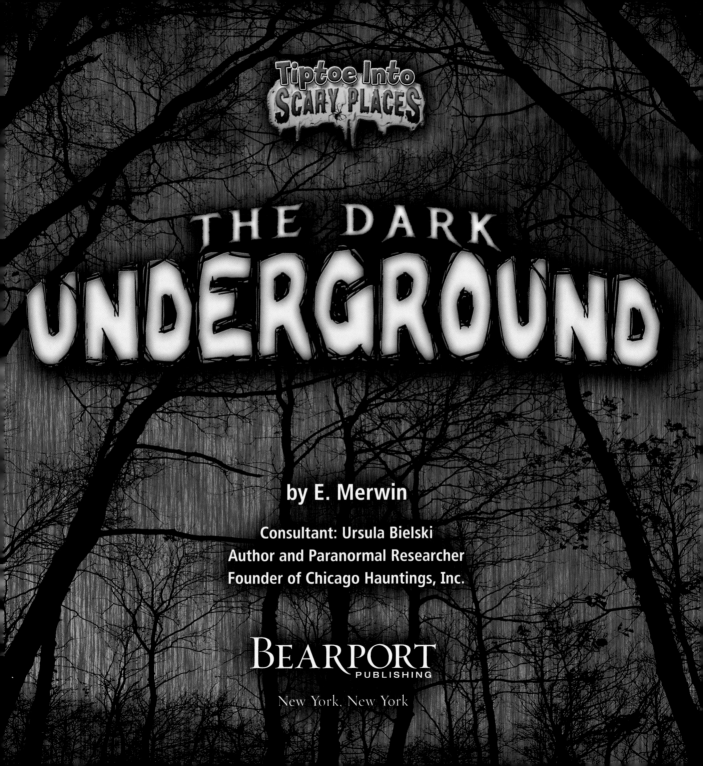

Tiptoe Into SCARY PLACES

THE DARK UNDERGROUND

by E. Merwin

Consultant: Ursula Bielski
Author and Paranormal Researcher
Founder of Chicago Hauntings, Inc.

BEARPORT PUBLISHING

New York, New York

Credits

Cover, © amskad/Fotolia, © Nicholas Pimola/Shutterstock, © EcoPrint/Shutterstock, © Pakhnyushchy/Shutterstock, © Jan Mika/Shutterstock, and © spaxiax/Shutterstock; TOC, © Jonathan Weiss/Shutterstock; 4–5, © ID1974/Shutterstock and © SvedOliver/Shutterstock; 6, © dmvphotos/Shutterstock; 7, © A_Dozmorov/Shutterstock; 8, © Everett Collection Inc./Alamy Stock Photo; 9, © yingko/Shutterstock and © Everett Historical/Shutterstock; 10, © photo.ua/Shutterstock; 11, © Everett Collection Historical/Alamy Stock Photo; 12, © Kamira/Shutterstock; 13, © Carlos Neto/Shutterstock and © Linn Currie/Shutterstock; 14, © Everett Historical/Shutterstock; 15T, © Brittany Erwin Photography; 15B, © twobee/Shutterstock; 16, © YesPhotographers/Shutterstock; 17, © i viewfinder/Shutterstock and © Donna Beeler/Shutterstock; 18, Wikimedia Commons/Public Domain; 18–19, © Stas Guk/Shutterstock; 20, © Carlos Caetano/Shutterstock; 21, © Stas Guk/Shutterstock; 23, © Pavelk/Shutterstock.

Publisher: Kenn Goin
Senior Editor: Joyce Tavolacci
Creative Director: Spencer Brinker
Photo Researcher: Thomas Persano
Cover: Kim Jones

Library of Congress Cataloging-in-Publication Data in process at time of publication (2018)
Library of Congress Control Number: 2017007500
ISBN-13: 978-1-68402-265-6 (library binding)

For more information, write to Bearport Publishing Company, Inc., 45 West 21st Street, Suite 3B, New York, New York 10010. Printed in the United States of America.

10 9 8 7 6 5 4 3 2 1

CONTENTS

THE DARK UNDERGROUND

You enter an **elevator**. The doors
shut behind you. Down the elevator
sinks until you're deep underground.
When the doors open, you see
something in the distance. It looks
like a young girl holding a candle.
She whispers your name. Will you
follow her into the darkness?

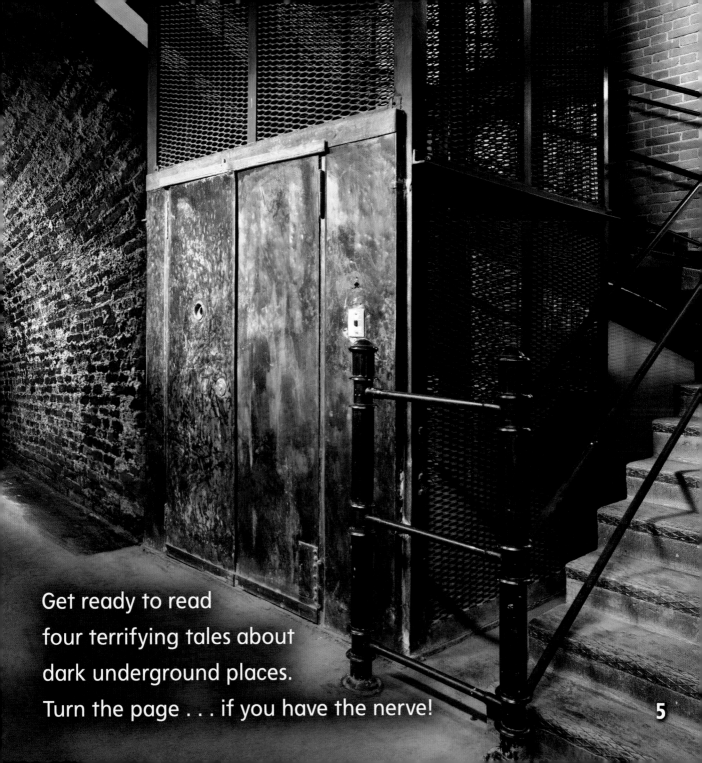

Get ready to read
four terrifying tales about
dark underground places.
Turn the page . . . if you have the nerve!

A Ghostly Secret

Jeddo Mine, Hazleton, Pennsylvania

It was 1904 in the town of Hazleton. Deep underground, coal miners pounded away at the rock. Suddenly, the ceiling of the mine gave way. The heavy stones struck a young miner, crushing him.

The other miners tried to help the **injured** man. They held him in their arms. The man's lips moved, but he was too weak to speak. Then he drew his last breath.

One year later, the men **descended** into the dark tunnels again. They had only the dim light on their helmets to lead the way. They gasped when they saw a shadowy figure. Its lips were moving.

Had the dead miner returned? And what was his deadly secret?

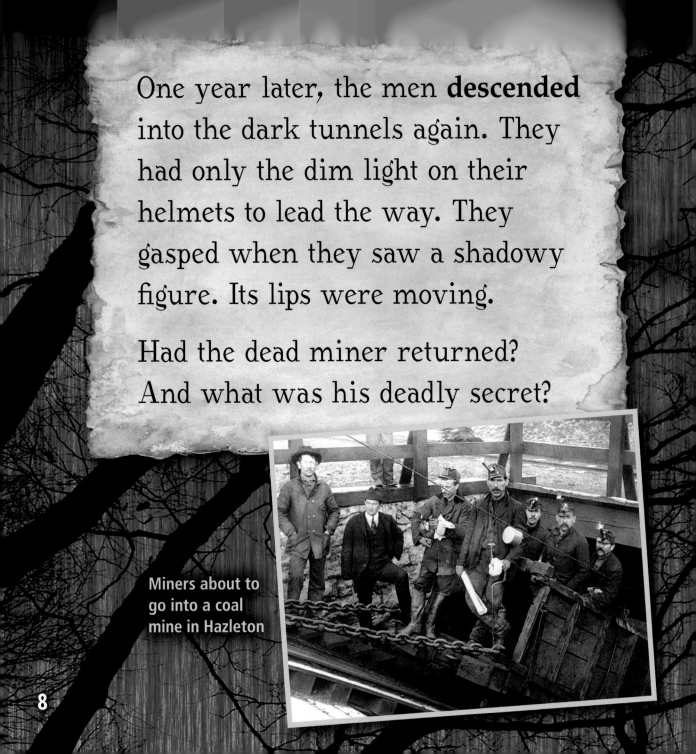

Miners about to go into a coal mine in Hazleton

After seeing the ghost, the men refused to return to the mine. Only after lights were hung in every tunnel did they go back to work.

PHANTOM DOG

Grand Central Station, New York City

There's a maze of tunnels under Grand Central Station. Every day, more than 750,000 riders wait for their trains there. But one unusual traveler may be waiting forever.

Grand Central Station in New York City

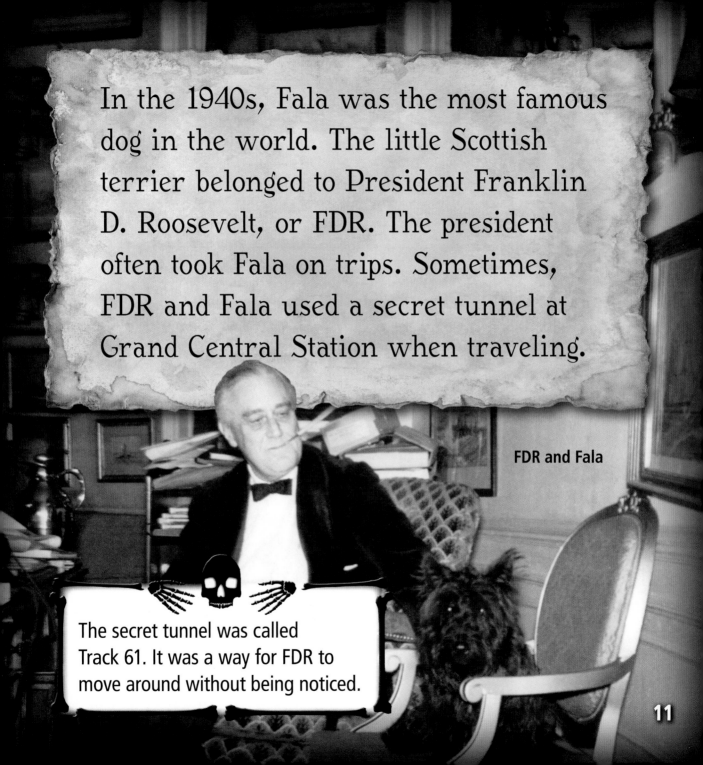

In the 1940s, Fala was the most famous dog in the world. The little Scottish terrier belonged to President Franklin D. Roosevelt, or FDR. The president often took Fala on trips. Sometimes, FDR and Fala used a secret tunnel at Grand Central Station when traveling.

FDR and Fala

The secret tunnel was called Track 61. It was a way for FDR to move around without being noticed.

In 1945, FDR passed away. It's said that minutes after his death, Fala let out a long howl. Then the dog ran off to a hilltop near the White House. There, he stared into the sky. Many believed Fala understood that his master had died.

A memorial to Franklin D. Roosevelt

THEY (WHO) SEEK TO ESTABLISH SYSTEMS OF GOVERNMENT BASED ON THE REGIMENTATION OF ALL HUMAN BEINGS BY A HANDFUL OF INDIVIDUAL RULERS... CALL THIS A NEW ORDER. IT IS NOT NEW AND IT IS NOT ORDER.

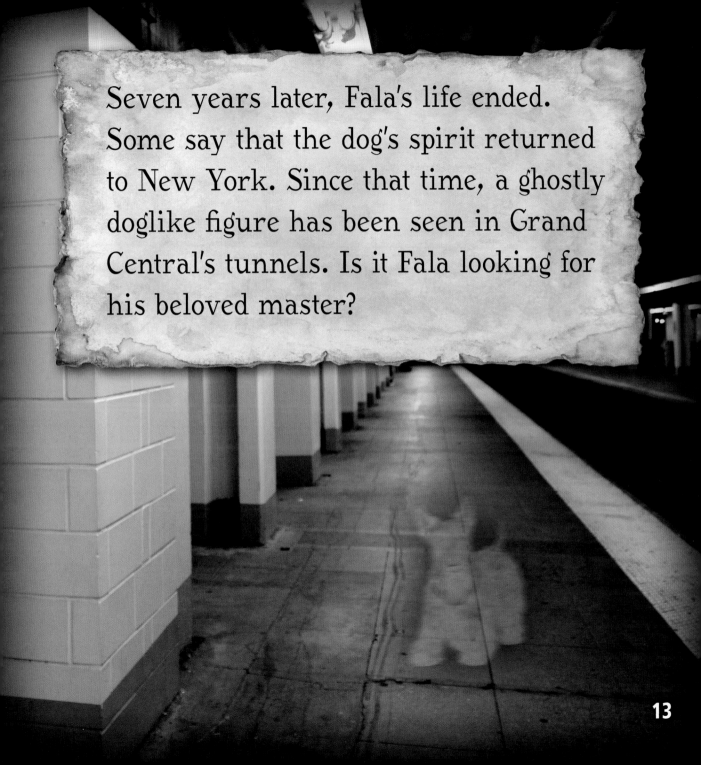

Seven years later, Fala's life ended. Some say that the dog's spirit returned to New York. Since that time, a ghostly doglike figure has been seen in Grand Central's tunnels. Is it Fala looking for his beloved master?

The Haunted Cellar

Hannah House, Indianapolis, Indiana

In 1858, a rich businessman built a **mansion.** It had 24 rooms and a secret **cellar.** The dark cellar was a stop on the Underground Railroad. At night, escaped slaves hid in the room.

The Underground Railroad was not a real railroad. Rather, it was a **network** of people who helped slaves escape to freedom before the Civil War (1861–1865).

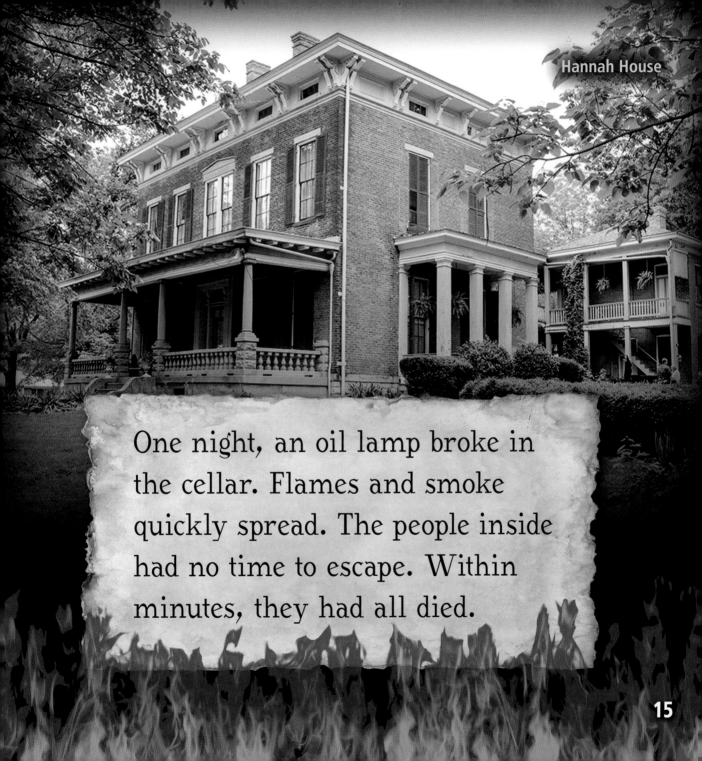

Hannah House

One night, an oil lamp broke in the cellar. Flames and smoke quickly spread. The people inside had no time to escape. Within minutes, they had all died.

Since the fire, whispering voices and moans can be heard in the cellar. Visitors often feel cold spots. They also see shadows believed to be spirits.

On the second floor of the house, doors fly open on their own. The ghost of the mansion's owner has been spotted on the balcony. Some say he's looking for the slaves he tried to help.

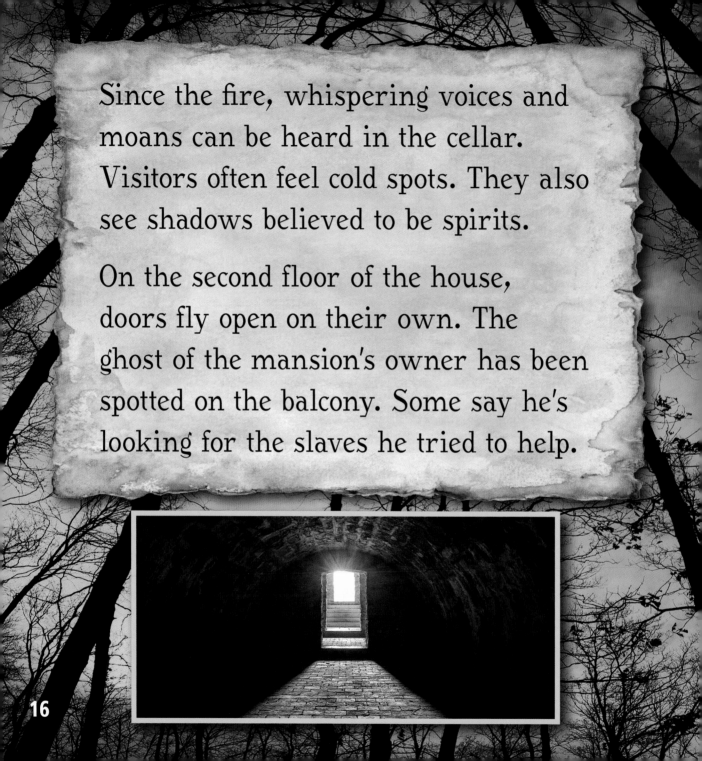

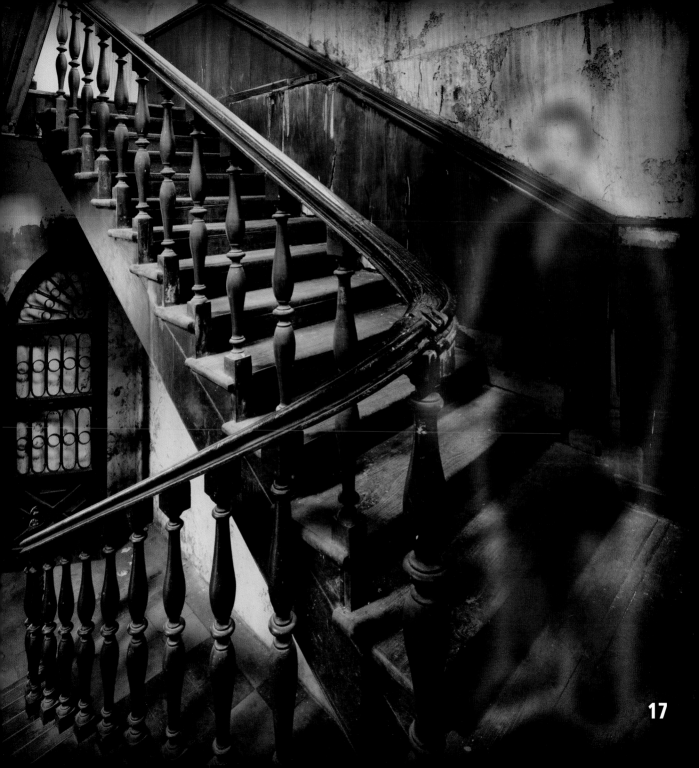

RUN FOR YOUR LIFE!

Catacombs, Paris, France

Under the city of Paris are 200 miles (322 km) of winding tunnels . . . filled with bones! More than 6 million people are buried in this underground maze.

In the 1700s, **cemeteries** in Paris became very full.

It took 12 years to move all the bones to their new resting place.

To make room for more **burials**, millions of bodies were dug up. Then the bones were reburied in **catacombs**.

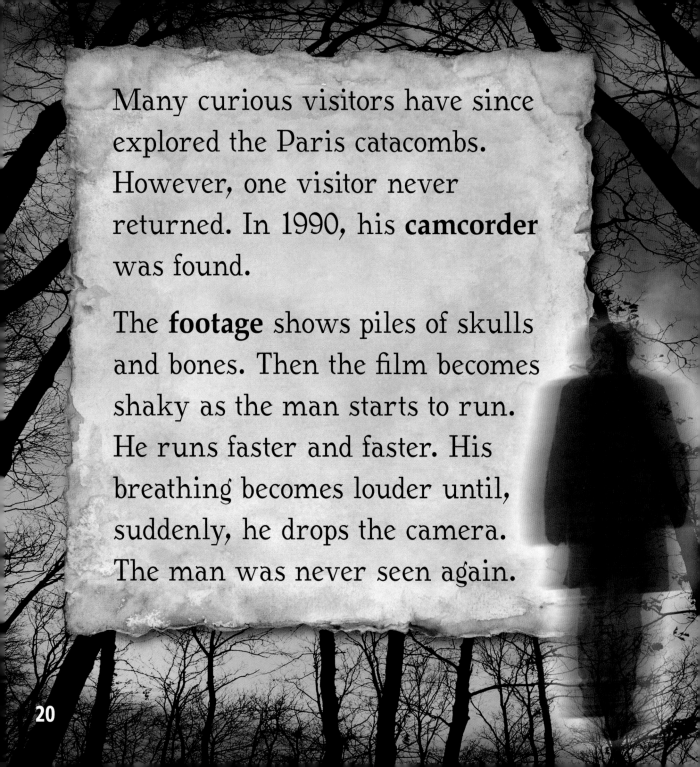

Many curious visitors have since explored the Paris catacombs. However, one visitor never returned. In 1990, his **camcorder** was found.

The **footage** shows piles of skulls and bones. Then the film becomes shaky as the man starts to run. He runs faster and faster. His breathing becomes louder until, suddenly, he drops the camera. The man was never seen again.

Underground Places
Around the World

HANNAH HOUSE
Indianapolis, Indiana

Descend into the cellar of a haunted mansion.

JEDDO MINE
Hazleton, Pennsylvania

Visit a mine where a ghost has a deadly secret.

GRAND CENTRAL STATION
New York, New York

Check out the station where a phantom dog roams!

CATACOMBS
Paris, France

Explore terrifying tunnels filled with bones!

Arctic Ocean

EUROPE

NORTH AMERICA

ASIA

Atlantic Ocean

Pacific Ocean

Pacific Ocean

AFRICA

SOUTH AMERICA

Indian Ocean

AUSTRALIA

Atlantic Ocean

N
W E
S

Southern Ocean

ANTARCTICA

GLOSSARY
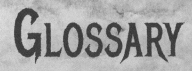

burials (BER-ee-uhls) placing dead bodies in graves

camcorder (KAM-kor-der) a small video camera

catacombs (KAT-uh-kohmz) underground places made of tunnels and rooms where people are buried

cellar (SEL-ur) a room below ground level in a house, often used to store things

cemeteries (SEM-uh-*ter*-eez) areas of land where dead bodies are buried

descended (dee-SEND-uhd) moved downward

elevator (EL-*uh*-vey-tur) an enclosed platform that goes up and down

footage (FOOT-uhj) scenes on film or video

injured (IN-jurd) when the body has been hurt

mansion (MAN-shuhn) a very large and grand house

network (NET-*wurk*) a group joined together

INDEX

READ MORE

Markovics, Joyce. *Chilling Cemeteries (Tiptoe Into Scary Places).* New York: Bearport (2017).

Rudolph, Jessica. *Ghost Houses (Tiptoe Into Scary Places).* New York: Bearport (2017).

LEARN MORE ONLINE

To learn more about the dark underground, visit:
www.bearportpublishing.com/Tiptoe

ABOUT THE AUTHOR

E. Merwin didn't believe in ghosts until she moved into
a house next to a cemetery in Queens, New York.
She has since moved from that house but still
remembers some spooky encounters.